BELIEVE TO LEAD

*AFFIRMATIONS AND REFLECTIONS
TO BUILD
EXCEPTIONAL AND EXCELLENT
LEADERSHIP*

DR. WYKESHA C. HAYES

Copyright@ 2020 KEEY PUBLISHING
Believe To Lead:
Affirmations and Reflections to Build
Exceptional and Excellent Leadership
By:
Wykesha C. Hayes
CEO of Keey Group, LLC
All rights reserved.

No part of this book may be reproduced, scanned, stored in a retrieval system, distributed or transmitted in any form or by any means—electronics, mechanical, digital, photocopy, recording, or any other-except in the case of brief quotations embodied in critical articles, or reviews—without permission in writing from the publisher. Please respect the intellectual thought, and creativity of the author by purchasing only authorized editions of this publication.

Published in the United States by Wykesha C Hayes of Keey Group, L.L.C.
www.keeygroup.com
wchayes@keeygroup.com

Paperback ISBN: 978-0-578-65828-5
Publisher: Keey Group, LLC
Printed in the United States of America
Cover Design: Ryan Lause
Cover Photo: akinbostanci/Getty Images/iStockphoto
Editor: Melody Gerard, Harmony Publishing

THIS BOOK IS DEDICATED TO

My husband Steve
My SONshine Zaire
My parents Beverly and Papa J
My sister Natalie and her tribe
My Daddy in Heaven Henry Lee
My endless circle of family and friends
You are persistent INSPIRATION

To those who live with untapped and an overwhelming
sense of purpose...
May you always DARE to BELIEVE TO LEAD

Thank you KEEY KOMMUNITY
I am FOREVER committed to the work!!

CONTENTS

Introduction 3
KEEY Approach: 10
Beauty in the Origami 12
Why I Chose to BELIEVE TO LEAD:
My Personal Breakthrough 17
I Am KEEY 22
You Are KEEY 26
We Are KEEY 29

SECTION 1: I AM KEEY 33
#iamKEEY 34
I am a LEADER: Curating a Strong Personal Leadership
Awareness 35
I am RESISLIENT: Self-Reflective Approach to Staying
the Course 38
I am CULTURALLY INTELLIGENT: Developing an
Ethics of Care and Cultural Appreciation 41
I am PRODUCTIVE: Cultivating a Strategic and Proficient
Mindset 44
I am a VISIONARY: Leveraging Communication that
Influences and Impacts 46
I am INFLUENTIAL: Leading through Influence 49

SECTION 2: #YOUAREKEEY 53
#youareKEEY 54
Your Safety is KEEY: Ensuring a Strong Privacy
and Protection Culture 56
Your Growth is KEEY: Building the Personal and
Professional Capacity of Others 59

Your Leadership Development is KEEY: Promoting
Goal Setting and Expectations 62
Your Resiliency is KEEY: Affirming Resilience in Others 65
Your Feedback is KEEY: Empowering the Voice of Others 68

SECTION 3: WE ARE KEEY 71

#weareKEEY 72
We Are PARTNERS: Harnessing a Culture of Partnerships 73
We Are UNIFIED: Driven by Transformative Vision 76
We are PRODUCTIVE: Examining Processes to Improve
Outcomes 79
We Are CHANGE: The Powerful Impact of
Exceptional Leaders 82
The Challenge of "WE": Anchoring Conflict as a
Growth Strategy 85
We Are BUILDING A LEGACY: Working with the
End in Mind 88

KEEY LEADERSHIP: BONUS AFFIRMATIONS & REFLECTIONS 91

Leading Heart Forward 92
Leading a Balanced Life 94
Leading Innovation 96
Leading with Confidence Above all Else 98
Leading with Emotional Control 101
I am WELL: Improving the Well-Being of Leaders 104
Leading in Uncertain Times: 107
About the Author 113

BELIEVE TO LEAD

*AFFIRMATIONS AND REFLECTIONS TO BUILD
EXCEPTIONAL AND EXCELLENT LEADERSHIP*

Welcome to the threshold of leadership. Your journey to redefining your leadership mindset. This book is a compilation of guided affirmations and reflections designed to develop strong, service-oriented leaders who value diversity, inclusion, resilience, and ethics as essential pillars for a strong leadership style. These transformative affirmations are intended to empower current and aspiring leaders who will undoubtedly experience challenges and roadblocks on their journey. **BELIEVE TO LEAD: Affirmations and Reflections to Build Exceptional and Excellent Leadership** leverages the fundamental principle of **SELF-TALK** and **SELF-VERBALIZATION** through affirmations and reflections to increase the effectiveness and confidence of today's **EXCEPTIONAL** leader.

    BELIEVE TO LEAD is poised to serve as a daily "leadership bible" to motivate leaders to shift their mindset, while maintaining a sense of self-worth during their journey toward leadership **EXCELLENCE**. Leaders will embark upon a reflective process of affirming their adequacy and worth with the ultimate goal of improving their practices, productivity, performance and profits.

    To the busy professional who is leading schools, organizations, corporations and within their personal lives, this journey is for you. To the eager aspiring leader who is looking for their big break, this expedition is for you. To the veteran boss looking to revitalize their passion to lead, this voyage is for you. This is your opportunity to affirm and accept the charge of leadership; understanding how vital of an opportunity it is to guide others forward.

BELIEVE
Verb

Accept (something) as true; genuine, or real

LEAD
Verb

To direct the operations, activity or performance of Cause (a person) to go with one by holding them by the hand, while moving forward.

INTRODUCTION

While this collection of leadership affirmations serves as an extraordinary tool for current leaders in professional settings, it is also designed to impact those aspiring to advance in their career, those daring to take on new challenges, those boldly leading projects or programming within their communities, and, on a more personal level, those simply wanting to move forward more exceptionally in life. I know these feelings all too well and the process of preparing for leadership or being a new leader in any environment can be difficult.

Difficult...but not impossible!

Perhaps one of the most pressing missions garnering my undivided attention are the ever-increasing gaps and disparities that women, especially women of color—face. I, like so many others, all too often internalize the burden of proving my leadership worth despite having reached the pinnacle of education in my field and having significant years of successful experience under my belt. What has and continues to sustain me, however, is understanding that leadership is not in title alone. I have reframed my language and have affirmed my own personal standards of excellence during my journey. What has manifested are experiences beyond my imagination simply because I focus on what I can control. Now, instead of affirming that excellence is the catalyst for promotion, I purport that exceptionality and excellence are simply the result of who I am. They're the language that I speak daily, and in this revelation, I believe, is the truest strength of a leader. This is the power in leveraging **SELF-VERBALIZATION** as a tool to maintaining and sustaining **EXCEPTIONALITY** on this glorious journey.

There are many leadership manuals and books that target leadership practices and mindsets, and, to that end, I wanted to provide a tool that was both inspirational and theoretically sound. Within the pages of this guide, you will find that I've turned leadership practices and characteristics into simple daily affirmations designed to shift perspectives, self-reflective practices, processes and performance.

I learned early in my professional and personal journey how much of an influence my thought processes have had on my success, even in the midst of uncertain times. For leaders, specifically, learning to manage our thoughts and controlling our verbal communication practice remains vital for **EXCEPTIONAL** leadership growth. These affirmations have proven significant in my journey, and I am certain that a large part of my ability to manifest great leadership skills is a direct result of my positively affirming who I am as a leader, how I show up, and what I want and need to accomplish regardless of any challenges. They have undoubtedly contributed to my awareness of maintaining a strong sense of emotional intelligence.

Exceptional leadership attributes transcend industries, careers, platforms, and cultures. There are some common characteristics that leaders possess, from Fortune 500 Companies to youth leaders in schools. **EXCEPTIONAL** leaders are self-reflective and devoted to growing. Quite simply, **EXCEPTIONAL** leaders carry **EXCEPTIONAL** values and the confidence to lead. Their mentality is different. We affirm ourselves in unique ways while helping others do the same!

One of my earliest self-affirming experiences occurred during my freshman year of high school when I placed third in the 400-meter dash in district finals, and I missed the opportunity to advance to regionals by just a lean. I was devastated!

I spent the next year training and visualizing myself in that district race over and over again. I can still remember the very poignant and firm pep talk I gave myself the night before the district race of my sophomore year. I began running that 400-meter dash in my mind. It was so vivid that I actually experienced physical symptoms! It was one of the earliest times I can fully remember embracing the process of hard work and the power of self-affirmation. I was going to advance...PERIOD. And I DID!

Since that time, I can tell you that every major event, accomplishment, goal or life-changing experience in my life manifested by purposefully shifting my mindset, seeing the finish line, and affirming that not only did I deserve to be in the race, I deserved to finish in **EXCELLENCE**. As such, committing to the work became organic but not without its challenges. With that said, I do not want to lose in translation the realness of my journey, nor do I want to illustrate a picture of perfection. This is not a Cinderella story, but it is a story of hope and faith that made pushing through every aspect of my journey worth it. This is my hope for you: that you become so infatuated with your power that you, too, will embrace your journey for everything it has to offer.

I do want to trace my personal journey back to my collegiate days at the University of Houston, because it sets the stage for my comprehensive experience in both leadership development and in the realm of diversity, equity and inclusion. As an intern in a national non-profit leadership program, I worked at a National healthcare Organization and a longstanding community organization that was dedicated to meeting the emotional, physical, spiritual and economic needs of its stakeholders. Both served urban communities by providing resources, services and programs through an inclusive lens. I gained a deep understating for applying DEI concepts to business operations, program implementation and relationship building. My mentors and intern supervisors both guided my experience as a future leader and made certain to set a strong foundation for analyzing the diverse needs of all stakeholders. After graduation, I carried these lessons with me into the classroom as an educator in the K-12 setting and beyond.

Capitalizing on these real-life experiences, I dove more formally into multicultural and inclusion frameworks by earning a Master's in Educational Leadership/Management and a Ph.D. in Curriculum and Instruction with a specialization in Urban Education. My research during both these experiences, focused intently on the perceptions, behaviors and practices of leaders in their roles as managers. These programs gave me a strong understanding of how others learn; while also developing programs that truly improves the practices of attendees.

The trajectory of my career evolved in unique ways; while simultaneously building Keey Group, LLC a learning and development firm. I have served leaders in small businesses, school systems, corporations, and non-profit organizations. I continue to facilitate each of these development opportunities with unwavering energy, clear examination of client needs, and a deep analysis of expectations. As I help clients establish comprehensive corrective action plans in the development of critical programs and processes, I also leverage trainings and learning experiences as an essential tool for leadership success. My premise for leadership development is to move the needle and help individuals mitigate risk in their daily interactions.

For the past 12 years, I have worked to establish myself as a reliable program and leadership development practitioner. I have trained 1000's of leaders as a professional, and consultant through the lens of multi-culturalism, diversity, equity and inclusion. I have presented to numerous national and international organizations, with an intent to help improve the functions of leaders in various capacities; and have presented keynote messages in most any capacity imaginable. As I've analyzed my work, I recognized that the overwhelmingly positive feedback from my interactions rest in three main areas. Leaders are 1. more personally inspired to change, 2. more equipped to support the development of individuals and 3. motivated to build more unified teams. None of which in my personal and professional opinion can be done without appreciating the value in being a self-empowered inclusive leader.

Particularly, one of the standout moments in my career was having had the opportunity to train 25 executive level leaders within a large grocery chain. Unpacking the components of identity and the implications of serving varying background of individuals is critical in developing the diverse lens of leaders. Identity serves as the foundation for improving the confidence and competence of leaders. As organizations across the globe become more intent on supporting leaders in their development journey, they must also learn that critical self-reflection is paramount. As an African American woman, I am able to rely on the authenticity of my own personal lived experiences as a way to connect and validate the research and studies I am diligently committed to.

In my vast experience serving hundreds of health care professionals, I have learned that there is an overwhelming need to foster inclusive and equitable environments among teams and patients. My research revealed that leaders did not have the tools or capacity to do this. Having worked with leaders for over 11 years, who served at the intersection of healthcare and education my research underscored a necessity for quality programs targeting vulnerable populations. My work evolved in the area of developing proficient professional development programs to fill the gaps for leaders. The multi-disciplinary approach to this transformative work, meant that I needed to support a range of team members, all leaders in some capacity to do what was absolutely best for clients. Leveraging coaching, advocacy, and communication skills among a number of competencies at the intersection of healthcare and education is perhaps my most groundbreaking contributions to the field of leadership development. In this space, I have helped design and deliver trainings around organizational change and influence, leadership fundamentals, bias, and diversity.

Another cornerstone in my journey is spending 10 years as lead chair and coordinator for a nationally attended professional development conference that provided a unique learning platform for almost 100 leaders annually. Every year, I pushed a team of professionals by challenging them to amplify the power of real world experiences and lessons. I executed strategies from the often scarce but latest research to improve conference workshops and activities for leaders. Year after year, attendees would return knowing that group and intimate opportunities for imperative discourse, hands on engagement and informative content would help them get it right in their spaces. In these instances, I led the charge in mastering the art of turning theory and frameworks into practice and application.

Though I can recall many more personally fulfilling moments over the course of my career, it is likely the work with service orientated organizations and companies that hold a special place in my core. It is these moments that I am reminded of the importance of the work. Serving as a speaker on Cultural Competency for the Girl's Scouts of America, or developing competency trainings for educators and school leaders at the local, regional and state level or helping hundreds of women develop strong businesses in the entrepreneurial space, the one leadership skill that is fundamentally transcendent across industries is learning how to strategically identify needs and manifest solutions that mitigate them. It takes inspiration, and a strong sense of self for leaders to push through.

So, from being a wife and mom to launching nationally recognized service projects, to completing my doctoral studies, while assuming leadership roles in corporate settings, I am one hundred percent certain that affirming my **EXCELLENCE** and producing **EXCEPTIONAL** outcomes is the most non-negotiable skill set I have learned.

This book is my purposeful attempt to push organizations and individuals toward the ultimate journey of leadership development. I have learned that while mastering technical concepts within our industries, businesses, community endeavors or through personal experiences, it is still paramount that, as leaders, we must also master the mindset of **EXCEPTIONALITY** and **EXCELLENCE**. This book is designed to shift your language, challenge your thoughts and redirect your beliefs regarding crit-ical aspects of leadership development despite the environment in which you lead. It is your ticket to improving what I call your **Powerful P's:** your practices, your productivity, your performance, your profits and your purpose.

The journey begins now, with your relentless commitment to engaging in this read, and understanding that you must first... ***BELIEVE TO LEAD.***

KEEY APPROACH:
THE PROCESS OF DEVELOPING EXCEPTIONAL LEADERS

After years of directly working with current and aspiring leaders across various industries, I began to identify shared attributes among **EXCEPTIONAL** leaders. Successful leaders remain open to transforming their practices and processes through continued self-development. They also demonstrate keen abilities for developing others, ultimately influencing the overall outcomes of the team. These leaders speak languages that affirm their power in developing within each of these areas. The language in this book is intended to do the same. It will affirm a language of **EXCELLENCE**, shift mindsets and promote improved practices of leaders whose goal is to continually perform **EXCEPTIONALLY** and in **EXCELLENCE**.

By leveraging research and personal leadership experience, I developed the W. C. Hayes KEEY Leadership Development Model for Exceptionality and Excellence. This leadership development model emphasizes a critical and transformative approach to improving the mindset and practices of leaders. Each section of ***BELIEVE TO LEAD*** highlights a critical element of the leadership development model. The first section is dedicated to the **#iamKEEY** tier, which encompasses the process of affirming personal development, personal accountability and critical self-reflection. It is the foundational stage that sets the tone for self-awareness and a strong system of personal leadership values. The second tier, **#youareKEEY**, places emphasis on developing and valuing others. Within this stage, focus is placed on guiding leaders through the process of promoting **EXCEPTIONALITY** within those around them. Essentially, people, sit at the core of the KEEY model illustrating that at the heart of an exceptional leader is a commitment to developing other leaders. The final tier, **#weareKEEY**, is the capstone of **EXCEPTIONAL** leadership development. This tier highlights process and performance improvement through the lens of team and community.

The W.C. Hayes KEEY Leadership Development Model provides a modular approach to leveraging experiential training opportunities for the sustainable development of **EXCEPTIONAL** people, processes, and performance. The goal of the model is to help organizations and individuals invest in utilizing a sound approach to improving the development of leaders.

To this end, the affirmations and reflections included in this book are written within the context of the W.C. Hayes Keey Leadership Development Model. The sections coincide with each element or tier of the model, highlighting proven characteristics, traits or practices associated with **EXCEPTIONAL** leadership. This is not an exhaustive list, but I have included those that have proven paramount not only in my personal journey but those that have proven pivotal in the development of leaders I've either studied or worked with.

Keey Leadership Development Model

**DEVELOPING SELF
(PERSONAL DEVELOPMENT)**
- Personal leadership skills (values and ethics)
- Self-Reflection
- Strategic Thinking
- Vision
- Cultural Intelligence

#iamKEEY

**DEVELOPING OTHERS
(PEOPLE DEVELOPMENT)**
- Goal Setting and Expectations
- Safety and Innovation
- Learning and Development
- Collaborate, Communicate, Connect

#youareKEEY

**DEVELOPING TEAMS
(PROCESS & PERFORMANCE DEVELOPMENT)**
- Cultivate Culture
- Team Development
- Diversity, Inclusion and Equity
- Process Improvement

#weareKEEY

BEAUTY IN THE ORIGAMI
A JOURNEY OF DIVERSITY, CREATIVITY AND INNOVATION

By nature, I am always intrigued by the beauty in transforming blank canvases into works of art. Given my amazingly non-artistic gifts, the physical manifestation of art work is not a readily accessible skillset in my toolbox; nonetheless, I am still moved by the spirit of art, creativity, and visual innovation, as is the case with this budding trend of artistic expression known as origami design.

The uniqueness of origami is its folding process; a practice rooted in Japanese culture. While this read will not delve much into the historical evolution of origami, its power lies in the transformative magic of converting a flat sheet of paper into a beautiful unique sculpture. I liken this process to the transformative power of the work embodied in this text and our ability as capable beings to **BELIEVE TO LEAD**. It personifies our fascination and frustration with complexity and our ability to do what seems complex while triggering a deep sense of confidence when mastered.

The apex of leadership development accounts for our unique experiences, our vast backgrounds, our cultural influences and how we maximize each of these imprints within our life to evolve as individuals and influential leaders. The value is in appreciating the dynamic variations that origami enthusiasts create, much like the varying leadership styles that we encounter and exhibit within our spaces. This excitement for artists and creatives transcends an incredible process of innovation, vision casting and self-reflection. It's the same telling journey of leadership development for so many aspiring and current leaders. The variations are all needed, all necessary to truly experience the beauty in the final sculpture...the end result.

Robert Lang, an American Physicist turned pioneer of origami art, offers a compelling intuitiveness into the mathematical influence of origami design. And while I'm also not a mathematical connoisseur, I am still greatly intrigued by the complexity of turning numbers, sequences, and thought processes into tangible products of beauty. Lang asserts that the same mathematical principles that allows one to turn a piece of paper into a folded masterpiece, is the same process by which complex real-world problems can be solved.

I am intrigued by the "difference" and transformation that results from each fold, each perspective, and each mathematical interpretation that ultimately contributes to the final origami product. Even with guidance and standard mathematical directives, the odds of perpetually creating an identical sculpture is nearly impossible. Perhaps it is this impossibility that intrigues others to engage in recreating and redesigning, attempting to repurpose blank paper into mockups of what has been designed before them. I'm not sure, but what I do know is that even in one's inability to replicate artistry, you often learn that difference rests in the reward of completion and growth, which is what you get in origami design.

So is the journey of leadership development! The approach and outcomes are almost always different, yet, those who fully value the process very much embrace the challenge of creating.

Leaders— **EXCEPTIONAL** leaders—are tempered by what was done before them but are driven by the power in diverse outcomes and so they fold and unfold based on their experiences aimed at providing a unique platform of beauty. The transformative process of "origami inspired leadership" can best be captured in this acronym:

O *Open-Minded*

R *Responsive*

I *Innovative*

G *Goal-Oriented*

A *Authentic*

M *Mindful*

I *Influential*

Of course, as an educator, I love to use acronyms, but as you continue to embark upon this journey, I encourage you to remember that, like origami, there is beauty in your uniqueness. Your approach may be vastly different but the outcome is what matters most. I want you to remember that this is your moment to create beautiful artwork. Included in this book is a blank sheet (both figuratively and literally). You have an opportunity to create; to fold the edges of your journey as you see fit. The process is often arduous, tedious and even complex, but well worth it for those who dare to **BELIEVE TO LEAD**!

I've yet to create the perfect origami artwork, but I keep showing up with new lessons to share, new goals, new desires, and new reasons why I keep showing up. This too is my leadership journey in the various spaces that I occupy.

I want you try your hand at this artistic expression and take an opportunity to personify your leadership philosophy through the process of origami design. What should you design? This is your choice. Technological advancement grants us access to some simple, and not so simple designs. Either way, I find this process to offer an incredible connection to the **KEEY** Leadership Development Model. I want you to choose a design that resonates with you and where you currently are in your leadership journey. Whether you choose to design a budding flower that resembles your potential as a leader, a bird that captures the freedom of flying beyond your comfort zone, a boat resembling shelter from the waves of challenges you may face, or even a hat that embodies the numerous leadership roles you currently serve, I want you to turn your self-reflective processing into origami art.

As you engage, I want you to retain a deep focus and comparison to your leadership development journey as it stands now. For me, I have also illustrated my personal philosophy in the O.R.I.G.A.M.I. acronym. Stay focused on the potential, the process, and the inspiration your efforts will offer those around you. Remain open-minded to the trial and error process of folding your life experiences into opportunities for exceptional leadership development. Travel through your leadership responsibilities as responsive as possible. Respond to the assignment, even if you do so with uncertainty. Leaders make decisions. Developing your leadership skills requires innovative thinking that awakens your ability to do what is necessary in order to thrive.

The complexity of leading in any environment is multi-faceted and in order to excel **EXCEPTIONALLY**, leaders must develop and maintain a goal-oriented mindset. It is truly the only way to advance. One goal at a time! O.R.I.G.A.M.I. inspired leadership illuminates one's ability to express adaptability. With every turn, fold, and direction, leaders committed to withstanding the difficulty of the journey will prove to be increasingly adaptable and agile in their efforts to complete the task. Every aspect of the KEEY Leadership Development Model requires leaders to be mindful: mindful of ourselves, those around us, and the robust process of working together. The beauty in it is the power to influence, inspire and impact as leaders; much like that which is accomplished by the final masterpieces of an artist. Both artists and leaders have the capacity to influence spaces, influence movements and inspire others. This is the beauty in origami. It is leadership defined...a process that dares one to ***BELIEVE TO LEAD!***

WHY I CHOSE TO BELIEVE TO LEAD: MY PERSONAL BREAKTHROUGH

THE INTERSECTION BETWEEN PERSONAL AND PROFESSIONAL fulfillment often produce feelings of scarcity or lack. It's the journey that carries this ironic sense of hope and discomfort all at the same time. While success may appear evident for some, the story of deficiency, stagnation, confusion, and unsettling instances of trying to understand gaps, distances, and differences still lingers...heavily. Too many times have conversations of struggle and bewilderment hampered the circles of humans, particularly within the spheres of women and people of color. These are the stories of professionals, with significant education and a myriad of experiences that, to the naked eye, would and should equate to both internal and external fulfillment. And yet, often times it does not.

In fact, in what I initially thought was simple procrastination in drawing this book to a close has turned out to be the greatest epiphany in its development. It is a startling reminder of the human story that quenches the soul of millions of women across the globe. It is the unsettling perception of a skewed reality: greatness and potential is in the eye of the beholder and not always within your professional catalog. The problem is that, too often, the eye that typically controls advancement is blind to the human greatness of far too many well educated, experienced and powerful people who remain stagnant by the underpinnings of what has long been overlooked within our society. And while the great minds of this world are offering a somewhat solution-driven response through the ever evolving processes of diversity, equitability, and inclusivity across every sector within every industry, the sting still exists. Significant work must be done.

The personal examples are many! It's the subtle— and not so subtle—reminders that while you've achieved much, your credentials are still easily forgotten. It's the daily struggle of executive level professionals who still feel the isolated weight of being the ONLY one at the table: the only woman, the only person of color, the...ONLY! It's the unmitigated, seemingly undeniable data that should substantiate **EXCPETIONAL** performance, yet you're still hammered with doubt, unbalanced monitoring, and never quite achieving the popular approval of the status quo club. And even more painstaking is the inability to be perpetually honest about the journey because the reality of these stories carry an unspoken rule: NEVER SPEAK ON IT OUTSIDE YOUR SAFE CIRCLES. Honesty is not easily appreciated, or, even worse, forgotten.

This book is the admittance of my reality. My reality is the reason, I dared—even challenged—myself to *BELIEVE TO LEAD* when retaining faith in my **EXCEPTIONAL** attributes seemed too much of a burden. It is the manifestation of my confidence in preparation for the big moments I'd longed for, both professionally and personally.

And, perhaps, much of the struggle lies in that admittance. I, like many others, bought into the notion that society has the power to determine my fulfillment, to create my **EXCEPTIONAL**, and to define what I deserved and how far I would travel. I was wrong. Very wrong. Thankfully, I have long carried a sense of resilience that erupted and interrupted every weight and struggle that society impressed upon me, especially in my most pivotal moments. That resilience was the nudge of hope needed, the moment that I knew I had to **BELIEVE TO LEAD**.

I have given myself permission to be a leader who recognizes and disrupts imbalances. I want to change double standards just as much as I want to transform the conversations within circles of unfulfilled women (and even men), I, unfortunately, have come to know all too well.

> *"I think sometimes women face the very real risk of not being seen, and not being heard, and so that's why I always tell young women, make yourself seen, and make yourself heard– this is your idea, this is your thought. Own it, express it, be the voice that people hear"*
> *– Loretta Lynch*

The greatest labor is the work that I had to do for and within ME. I had to rewrite my definition of fulfillment personally and professionally as a leader. My language had to shift, my voice had to change, and my story had to be amended for not only myself but for everyone that encountered the leader—that is ME! I had to acknowledge that **#iamKEEY**.

Perhaps the most fulfilling part of this journey for almost anyone who has overcome this societal sting is the growing affinity to empower others in spite of these challenges. It is the innate willingness to help create safer, more empowering systems for those who are in environments that deflate their **EXCEPTIONAL** daily. This part of my development emphasized my commitment to speaking more assertively and empathetically against practices that made invisible what otherwise are great examples of **EXCEPTIONAL**. I started to speak directly to those who, felt stuck and bruised by a system that discounted them before they considered them. I wanted to speak directly to the delay that many have and continue to experience by blazing a path for others to follow. I wanted to be the one set of eyes in the room that saw beyond what was presented and encouraged those whose light was slowly starting to dim because the unspoken toll was taking its course. I wanted to disrupt the battle between unconscious and conscious biases that created these feelings of isolation by, first, creating new expressions of self-talk and new mantras that countered any outcomes other than--**EXCEPTIONAL**. I wanted this process to enable me as a leader to speak directly and with certainty to the young professional that once was me. #youareKEEY.

At the end of all the great stories of heroism, lies this vision of "happily ever after". This is not easily attainable, but the happily ever after is the rise of the WE. The ultimate journey of leadership is to get to a space were WE will transcend the perpetual damage of deficits, separation, gaps, and unequitable systems and create a more productive and purposeful universe that values difference and uniqueness. When personal fulfillment is not subjected to what is gifted by others, we are no longer victims, and, instead, we become more focused than ever on arriving to the land of unity. The place where #weareKEEY

This drive toward profound self-awareness required me to show up when I didn't want to. It required me to still produce and find appreciation in the impact I made even when the acknowledgement was non-existent. I became less concerned with what was taking place around me and more concerned with my transitions within the spaces I occupied. I listened with a different ear when

I communicated with leaders who had seemingly broken barriers and reached the pinnacle. I learned from the stories of those who actually found hope in my **EXCEPTIONAL**. I forced myself into a space that found fulfillment in the experiences that rectified problems, created better lives, and saved others from discomfort. I learned to dance with those who held fast to the beats of integrity, and learned to love in a world of difference. With my limited artistic ability, I gave myself permission to create, to fold, and to manifest my complex experiences into evolving opportunities.

As a connoisseur of humanity, I often think about the great leaders that traveled before me, many of whom have had to sit in the most hostile circumstances, yet they still persevered with a focus on influencing others and making their spaces better. I relish in the commonalities of Harriet Tubman, Mother Teresa, former First Lady Michelle Obama, and Loretta Lynch, all of whom are statues of **EXCEPTIONAL** leadership.

> *"I alone cannot change the world, but I can cast a stone across the waters to create many ripples."*
> – Mother Teresa

This emphatically is what this process of ***BELIEVE TO LEAD*** is about! It is an infallible approach to lessen the ails of mediocrity and challenge both our internal and external communication, while simultaneously initiating a trickle down effect of empowered leaders who empower other leaders all while constructing more inclusive, productive and purposeful environments.

#IAMKEEY #YOUAREKEEY #WEAREKEEY
and we deserve to BELIEVE TO LEAD

I AM KEEY

You Are Your Best Thing
—Toni Morrison

Fresh out of college, I embarked upon my career as a teacher with no other goal in mind except earning a check. As a newly expectant mom, my law school dreams would have to make an abrupt pause. Slightly panicked, the exuberance from my core support system— my mom, sister and best friend—helped relieve some of the pressure. I was young, full of dreams, and a bit scattered, but one thing was certain: I had no intention of following my mom's footsteps into the classroom. A quick lesson in divine intervention takes place here...in this moment. God has a way of smiling at our plans.

That time period was perhaps one of the most critical in my life. I am not certain if it was the innocence of my fourth grade students, the compassion I often felt for a community that was stricken by so many unrelenting and systematic socioeconomic deficiencies, the pure love I felt from parents, grandparents and colleagues turned close friends, or even the unmatched feeling of being a new mother. I knew that while my best in the classroom was a lifeline for students, my core yearned to make a more far reaching impact. It was during this time that my inner voice and social consciousness became relentless in its pursuit to come forward.

Simultaneously, I began working on my Master's degree, and I began outlining the framework of what would become my non-profit organization and consulting firm. I needed a strategy and a fiscal road map to get me there. In other words, in order to build a business, I needed to replace my teaching income, so I launched into a global network cosmetics company, where I sold beauty products and grew a unit of over 100 women by teaching them business development strategies to help increase their earning potential. It was in this experience that I understood that the greatest power of a leader is having the opportunity to help duplicate other leaders.

I spent many evenings vision planning and journaling what I wanted to build. Dreaming about who and what I wanted to become became my afterschool obsession, as I sat alone in my classroom taking advantage of the creative air I'd created for students. I dreamed and I dreamed big, all while growing into my own as an educator, a person of impact—a leader.

In these moments, I built a reliance on a renowned spiritual strategy that exudes extraordinary professional practices, "make it plain upon tablets that those who read it may run". In other words, write it down. So I kept writing, journaling, and scribbling any and all ideas that were brewing within. Take heed to this message, because I have come to realize that all **EXCEPTIONAL** leaders are extraordinary at making the vision plain.

I was evolving as a person, and though I didn't particularly know it then, that innate leader that thrived as a school-age girl and college student was becoming a self-aware professional who longed to make a lasting impact in every space I encountered, despite the mistakes made and challenges I faced along the way.

Without these moments, I wouldn't have developed the skills needed to build me. Still today, I understand that in my pursuit to make an impact, I have had to define who I am as a leader and what that looks like when I show up in the environments I occupy. The notion, or theoretical principle, of self-identification was manifesting organically. I was growing confidence in my ability to rewrite the descriptions that were often used to describe myself and others that looked like me, such as "strong black woman."

This process of developing self, while coming to terms with one's deepest dreams, thoughts, and desires, is a non-negotiable. No way would I have ever been able to confidently articulate my vision for either my non-profit or Keey Group, LLC (at that time Keey 2 Kids &Teens), without coming to terms with who I was and wanted to be in the lives of my son, my husband, my students, their families and their community.

As my journey has taken several unconventional turns, I have realized that some spaces are much easier to engage in these self-exploratory experiences than others. External and workforce factors, relationships, and even poor leadership experiences will disrupt everything you thought you knew about your skills, your gifts, your goals, and yourself. It is in these moments that *the work*, as I call it, has to be done.

Doing the work in the most tumultuous of times builds intestinal fortitude and resilience. It has an uncanny ability to keep you focused on your road maps, even when the vision becomes too blurred. I am sure that you've been there—when your very existence becomes questionable, your career goals become foreign, your work environment is pestering, your role in your home and within your family becomes suffocating, and relationships become so perplexing that you question your own sanity. What do you do as a leader then? How many times must you come to the finish line and still not feel victorious? In these moments, you do the work to get better!

Today, leaders across every industry and within every facet of their lives are needing to take a step back and find safety in the air of their creative space. I've done this many times since those early years of my professional journey. There is power in embracing the **#iamKEEY** self-awareness phase and examining your development as a leader.

Examine how you respond when you don't get the promotion despite obviously being the most qualified, and the explanation is just as confusing as the actual act. Examine how you respond when your drive is marred by being called intimidating and told your goals are too far-fetched. Examine when you've given it everything you have, yet you still fall short. Examine your growth and how you respond in the face of a win only to find that you seemingly are the only one celebrating. It is in these moments that you dig deep, and you must still ***BELIEVE TO LEAD***.

As you engage in the first section of affirmations and reflections, go back to the beginning, revisit the warmth of a fresh vision— a budding idea, a new job, or new position, recognizing that before you become a leader for others you must, first, be a leader for yourself. Say it with me: **#iamKEEY**.

Now, Let's Do The Work!!

YOU ARE KEEY

*Success is only meaningful and enjoyable
if it feels like your own.*
— Michelle Obama

I GREW UP THE ELDEST OF TWO CHILDREN, AND WHILE I HAVE TO admit I may not have been the easiest big sister, I was always the protective, cheerleading sister who wanted nothing but the best for my little sister. I wanted her to be just as over-the-top and extroverted as me. Thankfully, in her calm manner, she remained steadfast in her own beliefs. She never did anything she wasn't personally interested in doing. As adults, we can laugh about it now, but unlike myself, who, for some reason, assumed that my being great was somewhat tied to doing and being what everyone thought I should be doing, she always created her own meaning. For as long as I can remember, she has never obligated herself to the expectations of others, especially if it didn't agree with her inner voice.

Not only have I always admired her for that, but, through our relationship as children and now as professional women with thriving careers, there is a benefit to cheering, supporting and meeting people at the point of their expectations and not our own. I learned to be her biggest and loudest supporter in the activities she chose to participate in and not the ones I thought she should. As the big sister, my role has always been to take every lesson I've learned and make sure that she embodied everything she needed to excel in her world, even if it wasn't as loud or overly consuming as my traits.

I've taken these lessons to heart, helping (as much as she would allow), supporting, defending, and protecting her. Today, she is absolutely the most successful and resilient woman I know, both professionally and personally. Hindsight is 20/20 but her best self-taught me a reassuring professional and personal lesson that undoubtedly confirms the depths of leading others. Leadership is less about directing and instructing, and more about leveraging the strengths and interests of those you lead to achieve success.

As I began to experience life outside of my immediate family, I have learned that true leaders are at their best when they are helping, guiding, and developing others. This is no less true for me today as it has been in my big sister role throughout the years. Pouring into others at my places of employment, within my community service organizations, and as an entrepreneur has become a purposeful point of emphasis for me.

Intentionality in the process of affirming the leadership development of others is just as important as affirming one's own personal approach to leadership. Our role is not to define how others show up but to empower them to tap into the power that resides within their core. In this place is their greatest ability.

As parents, siblings, community members, and professional leaders, our inherent responsibility is to gift others with the confidence to explore, engage, examine, and execute in a manner that empowers them. Leadership is truly the gift that should keep on giving. It is a shared responsibility that exists in all human interactions, regardless of title.

Think back to the leaders, role models and mentors that have made the most impact in your life. These people may have very well pushed you into uncomfortable situations or challenged you beyond your imagination, right? Now, reflect on how they made you feel. Did you glean a sense of care, commitment and trust from your interactions? I did! If transformation manifested a specific and unique feeling, I can unequivocally attest to the idea that every teacher, coach and mentor in my life invoked these same feelings within me.

As you examine and engage with the next set of reflections, I encourage you to focus on how you desire to show up in the lives of those you influence. What do you want them to both know and feel as a result of their interactions with you? This is not so much about you as it is about you learning the unmitigated value in communicating to people.... **#youareKEEY**.

WE ARE KEEY

"Teamwork is the secret that makes common people achieve uncommon results."
– Ifeanyi Enoch Onuoha

WHEN YOU CONSIDER THE MOST MEANINGFUL AND INFLUENtial moments in history, they all started with one person or a very small group of individuals whose vision sparked movements and trickle-down effects of mutual commitment. These historical innovators created avalanches of change by simply comprehending a fundamental principle: true success and true change is never achieved in isolation, rather it is a manifestation of engagements amongst a vision inspired collective. Exceptional leaders inspire engagement and vision!

Let's continue to unpack our model of **EXCEPTIONAL** leadership development. Leaders who **BELIEVE TO LEAD**, those committed to change, who are **EXCEPTIONAL** in their efforts value the unified efforts of an engaged team. This is the final phase of developing an **EXCEPTIONAL** leader, one who is uniquely able to galvanize a team that is committed to achieving an inspired vision.

Take Susan B Anthony and Elizabeth Cady Staton, for example. Their devout commitment to social reform and women's rights led to indisputable influence in the Women's Suffrage

Movement. In what would be a long-lasting voting rights struggle is known today as one of the most prolific moments in America's civil rights battle. Only a well-established, clearly articulated, and amazingly led effort could sustain decades of ongoing pushback, road blocks and challenges. Yet, today we are inspired by their vision and their commitment to bestowing the tenets of basic human rights. We are better and more courageous as a result of their example.

And while their efforts and the hundreds of thousands of contributors that joined their movements influenced much in the discussion of women's rights, we celebrate growth, realizing there is still work to be done. As such, we are now able to critically examine the approaches, characteristics, temperaments, and commonalities of the women like Susan B Anthony, and understand what it takes to carry the torch.

Today, leaders like you and I carry an enormous responsibility to inspire vision and carry forward a manifesto that mitigates the lingering gaps and disparities that still comprise the very best of who we are in our lives. What does it mean for leaders to diversify our tables in the workforce, champion for equal pay, produce leaders representing historically underrepresented groups, or build cultures were value is extended to all? It means that we need leaders who are not only expressly able to identify aspiring leaders, build their capacity, and generate movements among groups in a unified fashion, but one that also challenges self-indulging , self-serving mindsets that believe "I" is the end goal for the team.

This section is about merging the individual as a leader with the leaders they have developed and all stakeholders into one team, one culture, or one thriving group. At this stage, what we accomplish as a collective will reflect our unified values and the collective identity while still harnessing the beauty in each contributing leader.

As you navigate this pathway, focus intently on the power of team. Through these reflections, awareness at a global level should enrich your practices and commitment to appreciating the value in each contributing member of your community, lending itself to the development of a culture that embodies a strong sense of team... **#weareKEEY**!

AFFIRMATIONS | REFLECTIONS

SECTION 1:
I AM KEEY

#IAMKEEY

Say this with certainty:

#iamKEEY... #iamKEEY...#iamKEEY

The first set of affirmations reminds us that as a leader, our lived experiences, perspectives and philosophies are paramount to our personal development. They make us, mold us, shape us and impact the way we navigate. Taking personal responsibility for our development begins with awareness of who we are and making certain that we embody the very essence of some critical characteristics.

The first section of affirmations are personal. Read each of them as written in the first-person narrative. Commit to reflection and challenging your processes. Engage in the reflections, make some changes and embrace improvement.

Say it again: #iamKEEY...#iamKEEY... #iamKEEY

to developing the LEADER in ME!

I AM KEEY

I AM A LEADER: CURATING A STRONG PERSONAL LEADERSHIP AWARENESS

We should be motivated to step into our full calling as a leader of people and communities, conscious of our position of influence. We should commit to always using this awareness for the greater good of purpose, and vision. Knowing our capabilities and evaluating our limitations is fundamentally important to our continued success.

I understand the leader that is **ME**.

I appreciate my place, position and my purpose for existence.

I am not defeated by my thoughts, even when I question myself.

I value leadership wisdom that propels me into greater.

I am constantly examining my identity and how I manifest authenticity.

I am a brand that values my long-lasting reputation.

I transform doubt into the vision of change I am called to be.

I am empowered by the depth of who I am.

I am adaptable, optimistic, and transparent.

I capitalize on my strengths in my quest to lead **EXCEPTIONALLY** and in **EXCELLENCE**.

I am aware that my skill sets and knowledge are critically necessary and deserve to be shared.

I know what drives my emotions and choose to remain disciplined and composed.

I am pleased with who I am, who I am not, and who I am growing to be.

I understand that before I can **BE** for any cause, any person or anything, I must first **BE** for **ME**.

I am **KEEY**!

REFLECTIONS:

1. Reflect on your leadership journey and your progressive process of self-awareness, how have you evolved?

_____

_____

_____

2. On a scale of 1 to 10 (the higher the better), if you had to rate your feeling of self- awareness what would it be and why?

_____

_____

_____

3. Why is self-awareness important to your long-term development as a leader?

_____

_____

_____

I AM KEEY

I AM RESISLIENT: SELF-REFLECTIVE APPROACH TO STAYING THE COURSE

Resilience is key to the development of an exceptional leader. It is the spirit by which leaders are sustained, despite the hardships and challenges they may encounter. Being able to effectively bounce back, and rethink obstacles as opportunities will determine the true essence of a leader. Grit is the catalyst for moving forward and avoiding stagnation to ensure leading in excellence.

I lead from a place of strength, a feeling of courage, and an undisturbed space of resilience.

I clearly see my strengths and how important they are to my communities and relationships.

I am sustained by my power to embrace challenges and am continually adapting to conquer all stages of my journey.

I am a contributor of success, innovation, and growth because I leverage my experiences to master new stages.

I am not drawn to the negativity of a problem but to the power that lies in the new opportunities that evolve as a result of them.

I am continually transforming my thoughts and how I see failure.

I rely on a willful intention to learn despite difficult circumstances.

I am agile, a risk taker, and a change agent who is both self-assured and intentional.

I am not my mistakes, errors, or letdowns as my purpose is simply too important to be detoured.

I am focused, durable, strong and resolved.

I am open to the support of others, and leverage powerful communication to improve interactions.

I am a giver, a servant leader, and a caretaker of hearts—a leader who sees humanity in its purest form.

I embrace positivity and believe that this energy will define my leadership legacy.

I am **KEEY**!

REFLECTIONS:

1. List 3-5 challenges you've faced in either your personal, professional or entrepreneurial journey. What made these experiences challenging?

   _____

   _____

   _____

2. What skills did you use to help you overcome these challenges?

_____

_____

_____

3. What did you learn about yourself, and how will you continue to apply these lessons in your future journey?

_____

_____

_____

I AM KEEY

I AM CULTURALLY INTELLIGENT: DEVELOPING AN ETHICS OF CARE AND CULTURAL APPRECIATION

My greatest asset is to hear what I have never heard and feel what I've never felt while embodying a sincere respect for it all. Acceptance and appreciation for diversity are a reflection of values. In our roles as leaders, we should boldly and purposefully address intolerance by using empathy, compassion, and care as a fundamental approach to appreciating that which may be anomalies to us.

I recognize that culture is incredibly powerful and paramount to one's existence.

I am attentive to anyone or anything that disrupts an environment of inclusiveness and am prepared to challenge its stronghold.

I am not biased by statistics nor is my identity a representation of them.

I am capable of working effectively across generations and cultures.

I am growing daily to ensure a more grounded appreciation for multiculturalism.

I understand that diversity is the foundation for innovation and creativity.

I will seek to advance new perspectives, create spaces to learn, and normalize the realities of unique worlds.

I am a contributor to expansion, and I recognize that my appreciation for diversity makes me a universal influencer.

I embrace my entire identity and conceptualize, daily, the greatness my culture brings to my communities.

I am driven to meet the needs of that which I may not recognize through personal experience.

I respect all societies and will never require anyone to forfeit their greatness.

I am diversity. I am the embodiment of inclusion.

I am **KEEY**!

REFLECTIONS:

1. Examine the differences between cultural intelligence, diversity and inclusion.

_____

_____

_____

2. Think of a time you have had to rely on cultural intelligence to achieve a common goal? What skills did you use?

   _____

   _____

   _____

3. How does your upbringing contribute to your uniqueness as a leader?

   _____

   _____

   _____

I AM KEEY

I AM PRODUCTIVE: CULTIVATING A STRATEGIC AND PROFICIENT MINDSET

Productive and powerful leaders perform with purpose; while leveraging performance-boosting strategies to improve spaces. Being perceptive to needs and skilled at putting the right people in the right places at the right time for the purpose of effectiveness and efficiency is critical.

I create systems that drive performance.

I embed practices to improve outcomes.

I work at increasing efficiency, consistently exploring tech tools to improve automations

I disrupt chaos and confusion.

I value systems and protocols without being overbearing.

I document and deliver consistently.

I create possibilities by promoting innovation and creativity.

I am a master at delegating and organizing systems to improve performance

I pursue resources that I need to excel.

I articulate visions, expectations, and processes with clarity.

I am profitable, as is all that is influenced by my leadership.

I am a pillar of growth, innovation, and solutions.

I am **KEEY!**

REFLECTIONS:

1. What productivity strategies do you implement in your daily routine?

   _____

   _____

   _____

2. List the areas that you would like to improve in your personal, professional or entrepreneurial practices.

   _____

   _____

   _____

3. Reflect on your journey. How has your productivity influenced your performance?

   _____

   _____

   _____

I AM KEEY

I AM A VISIONARY: LEVERAGING COMMUNICATION THAT INFLUENCES AND IMPACTS

One of the foundational skills of an Exceptional leader is to master the art of communication and connection. Words are a reflection of who you are at your core, and who you want the world to know you to be. Say what you mean and mean what you say. Dwell in the power of language, being clear, concise, consistent, and constructive. When you speak, people will listen. When you listen, people are empowered. Allow transparency and authenticity to speak your truth and your message will build, develop, and lead.

I am adept at identifying when my tone or message is faltering, and I'm not afraid or too proud to adjust.

I will not counter my mistakes with linguistic folly. I will communicate lessons learned.

I will speak knowingly, honestly, and boldly in every mode I must deliver.

I communicate value and balance in both written and spoken communication forms.

I value the process of communication and understand all its parts.

I will maintain careful exchanges with others through behaviors, symbols, and signs.

My body language will help me convey messages of hope, clear expectations and transparency.

I am skilled at reading between the lines to examine needs, opportunities for improvement and growth.
I will use my skills to connect, to partner, and to support.
I will affirm with my words.
I will confirm with my actions.
I am **KEEY**!

REFLECTIONS:

1. Define your communication style.

   _____

   _____

   _____

2. How do you like for others to communicate with you at the professional, personal or entrepreneurial level?

   _____

   _____

   _____

3. What are your greatest communication challenges?

   _____

   _____

   _____

4. List ideas of improving communication within your professional or entrepreneurial environment.

_____

_____

_____

I AM KEEY

I AM INFLUENTIAL: LEADING THROUGH INFLUENCE

Leading through the complexities of change requires an undeniable commitment. The subtleness of leadership influence resonates with others and ignites a willingness within them to do without aggressive authority. Relying heavily on the power of persuasion and influence during critical moments of change is paramount in leadership. In exceptional environments, the power paradigm is replaced with tactics that are driven by influencers displaying innate role model behaviors.

I am a leader that inspires and meets my community in the trenches.

I elevate positivity through motivation and demonstrated production.

I lead with understanding and incredible concern.

My ability to Influence is matched with an unshakable sense of integrity.

My actions make me credible and poised.

I believe that people will follow what is sincerely authentic to them.

I welcome disagreement that pushes the team forward.

I embrace challenges and respect where varied insights will carry all.

I embody the confidence that creates an open and trusting environment.

I delegate with the objective of reaching all goals and creating sustainable efforts.

I leverage the art of persuasion with empathy and compelling discourse.

Recognizing that outcomes are critical, I apply strategic approaches and collaborative partnerships.

I am the essence of adaptability, high moral standards and transparency.

In this way, I am unwavering in my gift of influence because it truly is the source of success.

I am influential.... I am **KEEY**!

REFLECTIONS:

1. What strategies do you commonly use to convince, persuade or influence those around you?

_____

_____

_____

2. Reflect upon a time that change occurred and you felt it was poorly implemented, what could have been done better to influence others?

_____

_____

_____

3. What behaviors must you improve or develop to immediately improve your influence skills?

_____

_____

_____

AFFIRMATIONS | REFLECTIONS

SECTION 2:
#YOUAREKEEY

#YOUAREKEEY

There exists a fundamental priority for all leaders to develop EXCEPTIONAL and EXCELLENT leaders in an environment that values safety and leverages innovation. Exceptional leaders develop Exceptional leaders to improve and or increase their Powerful P's: practices, productivity, performance, purpose and profits.

Are you capable of articulating a collaborative message that speaks directly to each of your team members and future leaders? Have you made your interactions personable? Do your behaviors, processes, conscious and unconscious perceptions communicate to and connect with each individual?

Exceptional leaders are people-focused who possess an uncanny ability to pour into others and invest in their continued development through intentional goalsetting and learning and development efforts.

#YOUAREKEEY

Have you created, and or contributed to a culture that says **#youareKEEY?**

Are you speaking a language of engagement and sustainability to your team members and future leaders? A language that say's **#youareKEEY**

Do you contribute to a culture that says **#youareKEEY,**

Developing trust, leveraging their strengths and committing to their development while saying **#youareKEEY** reminds others that you are in the race with them.

This is not an easy process, but it is worth the journey. As you read the next section of affirmations, you will be pushed to empower, enrich and cultivate each individual on your journey.

#youareKEEY

YOU ARE KEEY

YOUR SAFETY IS KEEY: ENSURING A STRONG PRIVACY AND PROTECTION CULTURE

As a leader, engaging in proactive approaches will affirm the safety of people, first, and professional outcomes second. Without a strong sense of confidence, compliance is compromised and safe infrastructures are negatively impacted. Every effort should be made to establish and communicate safety expectations to your people.

Your confidentiality is sacred.

Your trust is a cornerstone of personal commitment.

Your privacy is unequivocally important.

Your safety, though among the masses, deserves individualized attention.

Your confidence in our culture is critical.

You are protected in this space with attention to your personal and professional safety and security.

You are protected when your decisions anchor success, and you are protected when your decisions result in opportunities to improve.

You are an integral stakeholder, and our culture serves as a safe haven.

Your confidence will never be compromised as it is your driving force.

Your information will not be breached in crisis, uncertainty or struggle.

Your access to data will never be denied so as to protect your ability to perform, ability to process and ability to produce, and in support of our commitment to transparency.

You can trust that a mutual respect that fosters success and exceptionality on all levels will serve as the catalyst by which we interact.

You are safe. You are secure. You are protected.

You are **KEEY**!

REFLECTIONS:

1. As a leader, how do you build trusting relationships with others?

   _____
   _____
   _____

2. In your current work environment, how are privacy and protection plans implemented?

   _____
   _____
   _____

3. When you think of improving privacy and protection practices, what role would you like to play? What areas do you think need improvement?

_____

_____

_____

YOU ARE KEEY

YOUR GROWTH IS KEEY: BUILDING THE PERSONAL AND PROFESSIONAL CAPACITY OF OTHERS

It will be a benefit to no one, if leaders do not establish cultures of growth and protection. Teams will work more comfortably in mistake free zones; otherwise it is impossible to develop. As a leader and partner in the professional development process, leaders should remain committed to preparing others to perform in **EXCELLENCE**.

You are a growing seed of greatness, and you are valued for that.

You are worth the investment of time, knowledge and mentorship.

You are wise in your choosing, careful in your planning, and committed to developing in your power.

Your areas of weaknesses are not irrevocable because with dedication you can transform.

Your strengths deserve your full confidence, as the culture will benefit from your offerings.

You are a big piece of the puzzle, and embody a brand that is uniquely you.

You should always embrace every opportunity to sit, listen and learn.

You work to fill your gaps, learn new skills and are supported in this process.

Your ultimate development is guaranteed because the leader in me wants to advance the leader in you and supports your voice in its ongoing development.

Your personal and professional development is KEEY!

You are **KEEY!**

REFLECTIONS:

1. What is your teams or organizations current philosophy regarding personal and professional development plans?

_____

_____

_____

2. How do you currently support your team members in assessing, developing, executing and evaluating their personal and professional development plans? If you do not, how do you foresee your efforts improving?

_____

_____

_____

3. Do you have a plan in place to achieve your personal and professional development goals as a leader? How can you personally improve your training and development efforts?

_____

_____

_____

YOU ARE KEEY

YOUR LEADERSHIP DEVELOPMENT IS KEEY: PROMOTING GOAL SETTING AND EXPECTATIONS

One of the most vital roles of an EXCEPTIONAL leader is to guide their people and emerging leaders in developing purposeful goals. Leaders should focus on goals that are purposeful, intentional and align with both the mission and their long-term desires. Expectations are mutually beneficial and serves as a critical role in duplicating like-minded leaders along the way.

You are an influencer and are willing to stretch.

You are disciplined and committed.

You are better today than yesterday and will be better tomorrow.

You are in control of your life's direction.

You are driven, and your goals are supported.

You are equipped to achieve success in all that you do.

You are growth epitomized and destiny in development.

You are exactly what is needed on this journey.

You are intentional and strategic in developing your goals.

Your plans are productive, proficient and powerful.

You are naturally engaging, skillfully sound, and analytically advanced.

You are creative, and your contributions have not gone unnoticed.

You have permission to thrive and succeed as it is to the benefit of all those around.

You are a difference maker and lives will be changed because of it.

You are on track. You are the voice of difference. You are open to the challenges of growth.

You are **KEEY**!

REFLECTIONS:

1. What characteristics do you, as a leader, most appreciate in a leadership mentor?

   _____

   _____

   _____

2. What characteristics have you, as a leader, not responded well to when you fall short of achieving a goal or meeting expectations?

   _____

   _____

   _____

3. In what ways can you reward others for achieving their goals?

_____

_____

_____

YOU ARE KEEY

YOUR RESILIENCY IS KEEY: AFFIRMING RESILIENCE IN OTHERS

Although they may face overwhelming responsibilities, your team or organization should unequivocally understand that they exist in a space created to nurture positivity and consideration. Just as important as individual resilience is, so is intentionally developing and promoting bounce back in others. Empowering perseverance in others is KEEY:

You are stronger than your past experiences and any personal or professional challenges you may face.

You are socially and emotionally equipped.

You are prepared, creative, and innovative.

You are tempered enough to manage difficult decisions and situations admirably.

You are encouraged to take great care of you, for you are important.

You will continue to show up in the face of challenges and uncertainties.

You will face changes with a level head and responsible dealings.

You are encouraged to chase your fears until you master its stronghold.

You are steadfast and open to your potential, so be kind to yourself.

You are mindful of self-appreciation and lead with that same energy.

You cherish those that support you and celebrate your wins graciously.

You move in a positive spirit and are conscious of how infectious you truly are in this space.

You master your goals, exceed expectations, and impact lives abundantly.

You are a performer. You are productive. You are profitable.

You are **KEEY**!

REFLECTIONS:

1. Think of a time when you've had to help someone restore their self-efficacy.

_____

_____

_____

2. What strategies have you used to help build confidence in others?

_____

_____

_____

3. How do you contribute to a "mistake-protected" culture?

_____

_____

_____

YOU ARE KEEY

YOUR FEEDBACK IS KEEY: EMPOWERING THE VOICE OF OTHERS

The cornerstone of long-lasting relationships is rooted in three fundamental principles: collaboration, communication and connection. When leaders cultivate opportunities for feedback, they are essentially empowering the voice of others to play a pivotal role in advancing the mission of the whole. It is in these opportunities that leaders promote the shared responsibility of leadership-irrespective of title. This level of empowerment is **KEEY**.

Your voice is an integral part of the process and critical to the team.

Your ideas should be shared without fear of failure and retaliation.

You have the authority to be you and communicate in a manner that uplifts others.

Your voice is evidence of your authenticity and the depths of your skills.

You should be comfortable giving timely correction and critique, for this refinement is what makes the system unique.

You are encouraged to remain thoughtful and consistent.

Your ability to assess and examine is powerful, valuable, and an effective approach to growth.

Be committed to improving performance and productivity around you daily.

You should remain mindful of the influence that you have and the impact that you can make.

Your words are a source of connection and will ultimately define your legacy.

Express your sincere perspectives, progressive ideas and your keen insights.

You are **KEEY**!

REFLECTIONS:

1. Reflect upon an environment in which feedback was welcomed. What did you learn?

   _____

   _____

   _____

2. Why is feedback important to the process of improvement and growth on your team or in your organization? What is your personal communication mantra?

   _____

   _____

   _____

3. Given the environment in which you currently serve, assess your feedback system. How can this system improve and list three ways you can encourage open feedback.

_____

_____

_____

AFFIRMATIONS | REFLECTIONS

**SECTION 3:
WE ARE KEEY**

Now that you've grown accustomed to building and improving personal and targeted relationships, the next journey is to preserve the unity of your team, your stakeholders and yourself.

#WEAREKEEY

Every decision made, every policy analyzed, every aspect of operations or programming must communicate a singular tune.

The affirmations and reflections in this section will force you to acknowledge the challenges of partnerships, appreciate the common mission, and reflect upon the long-term implications of a unified team.

Are you ready? Are you ready to cultivate a culture of **EXCELLENCE?** Are you ready to develop healthy team dynamics? Are you ready to leverage diverse teams, inclusive approaches and equitable processes? In doing all this, are you ready to improve team functions and processes to achieve **EXCEPTIONALITY?**

#WEAREKEEY

WE ARE KEEY

WE ARE PARTNERS: HARNESSING A CULTURE OF PARTNERSHIPS

When everyone truly matters, partnerships will serve as a strong foundation for team focused organizations. There is no "I" in this journey that is stronger than the collective. The strength of an operations work will always be defined by the lives that are impacted and influenced...from our leaders to our clients and every contributor in between. The power of partnerships is inevitably the lifeline of continued success.

We work empathetically, compassionately, and carefully... always mindful of people and their needs.

Shifting our perspectives toward a collaborative and community model is the essence of growth.

Our stamp of approval comes from our clients, as they are the ultimate measure of productivity.

We show up appreciating our differences and embracing our commonalities as a unit.

We value every voice and benefit from the multifaceted levels of skills upon us.

We fully recognize the role that external and internal stakeholders play.

We make decisions and demands of ourselves because we are aiming to influence.

Every decision we make is in response to the demands of those we serve.

We are strategic in solving problems, and exceptional in addressing complex challenges.

We foster opportunities to expand our expertise, and groundbreaking perspectives.

Collectively and collaboratively... We are **KEEY**!

REFLECTIONS:

1. Identify your stakeholders at every level and evaluate your engagement process with each of them as a leader.

   _____

   _____

   _____

2. What is your "collaborative" team philosophy?

   _____

   _____

   _____

3. How do you measure success as it relates to impacting or influencing your people?

_____

_____

_____

WE ARE KEEY

WE ARE UNIFIED: DRIVEN BY TRANSFORMATIVE VISION

It is each of our responsibility to remain mindful of the goal, mission, vision, and values that unify us. We uphold the power of vision, commitment to high standards and moral intuitiveness that guide us. As a body of conscious leaders, our collective essence rest in our ongoing pursuit of manifesting extraordinary and transformative vision.

Our vast abilities are drivers in our journey toward excellence. We are enthusiastic pacesetters in this organizational fortress.

Our differences, though striking, are bound by many common things such as our personal values and caring mindset.

Our dynamic and effective approach inspires and promotes success.

Our persistence is molded by our teams' commitment to truth, passion, and transparency.

Our fundamental goals to serve, achieve, and thrive are drivers of our innovation, creativity, and wisdom.

We are the essence of a vision united by which we commit daily.

We curate opportunities bigger than ourselves to ensure that vision is purposefully fulfilled.

Our vision is regularly communicated, insightfully implemented and relentlessly pursued.

We are purposeful, productive and profitable.

We are change agents, leaders and exceptional performers.

We are the end result of effort, focus and sheer determination.

We are **KEEY**!

REFLECTIONS:

1. What is the mission, vision, and goal of your organization? How do you communicate this message both directly and indirectly?

   _____

   _____

   _____

2. Evaluate your current approach to developing team unity. How do you involve others in the goal-setting process?

   _____

   _____

   _____

3. It is imperative that each team member is aware of team members' strengths as vision is emphasized. How do you build this level of aligned awareness?

_____

_____

_____

WE ARE KEEY

WE ARE PRODUCTIVE: EXAMINING PROCESSES TO IMPROVE OUTCOMES

Success is measured by our performance, the change we create. We measure it by what we achieve and produce, so our processes should always improve to keep us perfectly positioned. When your services are widely effective, your efforts are influential, your impact is far reaching, and your reputation is impeccable.

We are trailblazers, setting the stage for exceptional outcomes.

We are innovators, creating outstanding products.

We are trusted because we are marked by intelligence and sound judgement.

We increasingly retain team members, and we overcome the challenges faced by our markets.

We are profitable and performance-driven.

We are socially conscious and aware of the needs of our community.

We demand and are driven to deliver excellence.

We continually emphasize our presence and growth.

We understand to arrive at our destination innovation and clarity is necessary.

We build the capacity of our organization and our people when we perform in excellence.

We are dedicated to winning with integrity, realizing that it benefits us all.

We push until the finish line is behind us and even still we are preparing for the next lap.

We strive to maintain. We strive to improve and we strive to retain all that we accomplished.

We show up daily, not simply to exist but to excel.

We are **KEEY**!

REFLECTIONS:

1. How do you evaluate performance, productivity, and profit outcomes? How often?

   _____

   _____

   _____

2. What are your current services, programs and or products? If you don't have any create a list of ideas that you would like to offer your stakeholders as a leader.

   _____

   _____

   _____

3. What do you want your stakeholders to learn after engaging with your products or services?

   _____

   _____

   _____

WE ARE KEEY

WE ARE CHANGE: THE POWERFUL IMPACT OF EXCEPTIONAL LEADERS

The ever evolving impact of change remains a critical focus of leaders in a multitude of sectors. Beyond presenting unified messages, leaders must understand how to effectively support the collective through simple and complex change experiences. Change is not only inevitable but it is necessary despite often times carrying fear induced stigmas.

Change will drive us to new levels of greatness.

Change is the opportunity for renowned innovations and critical self-reflection.

Change will not impede our commitment to vision, we will make certain of it.

We will sustain with clear and compelling communication.

We will manifest expectations on the backs of strategic planning.

Change, though scary will energize us as a
team. How we manage change will define our
legacy. Change will not break us.

Change will not stifle our growth.

We will learn and we will develop individually and collectively.

We will identify our priorities and approach our efforts positively.

We will harness feedback in our drive for exceptional outcomes.

We will build upon the intellect of every stakeholder.

We will reconcile challenges and nurture relationships in every capacity.

We are ambassadors of change, willing to move forward in the face of uncertainty.

Change is our oyster and the world is our stage.

We are KEEY!

REFLECTIONS:

1. How comfortable are you leading in the mist of expected and unexpected change?

   _____

   _____

   _____

2. What strategies do you rely on to motivate and inspire those around you during change?

   _____

   _____

   _____

3. How do you leverage collaboration during change?

_____

_____

_____

WE ARE KEEY

THE CHALLENGE OF "WE": ANCHORING CONFLICT AS A GROWTH STRATEGY

The heart of our team is defined by the challenges we overcome. We overcome any challenges by our ability to communicate differences, but these challenges serve as the foundation of growth instead of hindering us. Complexity will not consume us but will instead ignite collaborative relations.

We handle the inevitableness of conflict with dignity and empathy.

We will not allow disengagement and frustrations to overwhelm us or stifle our end results.

We will embrace clarity and trust in times of uncertainty.

We remain focused on our roles and respect the diversity among us.

We remain committed, strong and forthcoming as leaders.

We remain morally conscious and benefit from the stumbles we face.

We remain committed to developing the skills needed to thrive even in the face of adversity.

We analyze our workflow and processes to ensure success.

We will push in the face of struggle instead of sowing into defeat.

We will not bow down or succumb to drama, negativity or unprofessionalism.

We will disengage or terminate conflict that refuses to diffuse by its own will.

We will be strengthened by our challenges, trusting that innovation is within arm's reach.

We will assume positive intentions and learn to be stronger communicators.

We will chart better roads as a result of our dedication to pushing through.

We will leverage restraint and create an environment of support.

We are **KEEY**!

REFLECTIONS:

1. What is your philosophy regarding conflict resolution?

_____

_____

_____

2. What essential characteristics do leaders need to manage team challenges?

_____

_____

_____

3. What role should leaders play in helping teams/individuals overcome challenges?

_____

_____

_____

WE ARE KEEY

WE ARE BUILDING A LEGACY: WORKING WITH THE END IN MIND

When the doors close and the journey is written, will our story stand? While what we do today is often tasked, our imprint should last for infinity. Teams built together, will do great things together and this is how we'll be known. Understanding that yesterday is a foundation for today's efforts and tomorrow's legacy, we will journey beyond the now to solidify our greatness.

We will prevail beyond our years because our legacy is that of a team united.

We will serve the greater good and impact lives because of what we accomplish together.

We will become individually exceptional because our collective effort is a powerful force.

We are transparent and transformative.

We are viable and durable.

We are productive and strong.

We are innovative and prudent.

We are solving the challenges of today and those anticipated for tomorrow.

We are impactful and trustworthy.

We are producers and profitable.
We are difference makers and creators of opportunity.
We have an imprint that will last forever.
We are **KEEY**!

REFLECTIONS:

1. What legacy do you want to leave as a leader?

   _____

   _____

   _____

2. What legacy do you want your team to leave?

   _____

   _____

   _____

3. What legacy-building activities do you or can you do as a team to help influence the overall mindset of your team?

   _____

   _____

   _____

KEEY LEADERSHIP: BONUS AFFIRMATIONS & REFLECTIONS

"I've learned people will forget what you said, people will forget what you did, but people will never forget how you made them feel."

– Maya Angelou

KEEY LEADERSHIP

LEADING HEART FORWARD

A servant's heart will never steer you wrong. It will always guide you toward the most comprehensive, yet compassionate solutions available. When one embodies an ethical mindset that considers impact and influence, heart-forward leadership is maximized. Leadership driven by the heart is more than a manifesto. It is a principle that is paramount to success.

My leadership is a direct reflection of who I am as a person.

At the heart of my approach is compassion and concern for others.

I will frame all my dealings with ethics.

I am driven by human relations.

I will never lead above the implications of mankind.

I will be transformational, transparent, and timely in my dealings.

I will remain empowered by my vested interest in others.

I align all my efforts with my established values and
morals. I will advocate for right and mediate with
sincerity.

I will listen with respect, appreciation, and support.

In all that I do as a leader, my heart will remind me that I am KEEY... You are KEEY...We Are KEEY!

REFLECTIONS:

1. Develop a list of morals and values that are important to you as personally and professionally.

   _____

   _____

   _____

2. What does a "people-first" leadership mentality mean to you?

   _____

   _____

   _____

3. List characteristics of a "heart forward" leader.

   _____

   _____

   _____

KEEY LEADERSHIP

LEADING A BALANCED LIFE

Balanced living is the cornerstone of success. Family, friends, and support systems are all deserving of our best selves, because without them, professional achievement results in false fulfillment. Living in balance totally and completely supersedes all other obligations.

I am driven by my personal and professional desires.

Yet, I understand fully the difference between the two.

I value growth, while, sustaining an appreciation for those that mean the most to me.

I center my thoughts daily on what truly matters when all else fails.

And am truly empowered by simply having the opportunity.

I will meditate on those things that enrich my life with positivity,

As, my family, my friends and those I serve are among them.

I will remain complete and attentive to the needs of my soul at all times.

I am complete, ensuring those around me are motivated to experience the same.

Spiritual fulfillment is a gift that I leverage daily.

I am balanced, happy and whole, so those around me are balanced happy and whole.
Balance is the **KEEY**.
I am **KEEY**...You are **KEEY**...We are **KEEY**!

REFLECTIONS:

1. Do you firmly believe you are living a balanced life? Explain.

   _____

   _____

   _____

2. Create a list of things and people that you would like to give more attention to.

   _____

   _____

   _____

3. Do you have designated times to simply reflect? What do you enjoy doing most?

   _____

   _____

   _____

KEEY LEADERSHIP

LEADING INNOVATION

Innovative leaders present groundbreaking ideas, and are driven by solutions and systematic approaches to improvement. Through experimentation and exploration, innovative leaders leverage teams to make decisions. With determination, willpower, and an openness to diversity of thought, we can increase knowledge, improve outcomes and shrink complexities.

I am free-thinking and original.

I identify challenges and pain points all while seeking change.

I examine leadership processes and maintain a proactive mindset.

I am positioned outside the box; with a skill for exploring the unknown.

I work diligently to improve strategic processes.

I am continually learning, developing clarity and maintaining focus.

I am progressive and refined with a simple end goal in mind: to be impactful, innovative, and a game-changer.

I am excited by new.

I attract groundbreaking ideas and produce breakthrough outcomes.

I am empowered by different.
I am driven by exceptional.
I am **KEEY**!

REFLECTIONS:

1. Define innovation. How do you contribute to developing an innovative culture?

2. As a leader, in what ways do you personally approach boosting your innovative spirit?

3. Describe your most innovative program, project, or service. What qualifies this as unique and innovative?

KEEY LEADERSHIP

LEADING WITH CONFIDENCE ABOVE ALL ELSE

Zeal and a go-getter energy are magnets for success. Often referenced as "executive presence," confidence drives ambition and a leader's intuitiveness. We must remain confident in our ability to develop a collaborative culture, with a compelling voice, and a clear vision, while maintaining focus and avoiding distractions.

I am not defined by perceptions and will not shrink to fit them.

I am deserving of every opportunity I have to lead.

I am confident in my ability to build capacity in others.

I am confident in my training, skills and knowledge.

I am poised and self-assured in my strengths and courageous enough to build upon my weakness.

I am a confident risk-taker, fearless galvanizer, and I am results-oriented.

I am efficient, effective and interpersonal.

I am different, diversity in the flesh, and I am powerful.

I am everything needed to shift cultures.

I create greatness.

I am born to be a leader and I belong in any space at any time opportunity presents.

I am **KEEY!**

REFLECTIONS:

1. Reflect on your greatest leadership qualities. What are they and how do they benefit the environments you serve?

   _____

   _____

   _____

2. What is your greatest leadership moment and why?

   _____

   _____

   _____

3. Thinking beyond any limits, what are your wildest leadership dreams?

   _____

   _____

   _____

4. What valuable lessons have you learned on your leadership journey?

_____

_____

_____

KEEY LEADERSHIP

LEADING WITH EMOTIONAL CONTROL

As a leader, we are to remain calm and adjusted, accurately communicating our feelings. Situations change often, b ut change should not irritate performance, hinder productivity, nor entice the unruly treatment of others. Emotionally sound leaders create peaceful environments, which are psychologically safe and epicenters for self-aware existence.

I am a master manager of my emotions.

I recognize the powerful impact that evolves as a result of healthy interactions.

I am incredibly self-aware and consciously attentive t o my responses.

I understand that emotional control is paramount, and I subscribe to the importance of teaching others to do the same.

I am attentive t o t hose around me, t heir personality, their interactions and behaviors.

I will not operate in a state of defensiveness and will contribute to a supportive environment.

I am not easily offended and release myself from my mistakes.

I will always allow others to recover.

I will give without strings attached.

I will judge a person's character with a sincere heart and react responsibly.

I am emotionally strong.

I always work to improve.

I am **KEEY**!

REFLECTIONS:

1. Conflict is inevitable. What process do you follow to control your personal emotions in intense situations?

　　_____

　　_____

　　_____

2. Define emotional intelligence. Have you engaged in any formal E.I. training?

　　_____

　　_____

　　_____

3. Why is it imperative that you understand the impact of developing high E.I.?

_____

_____

_____

4. Examine your emotional triggers, identify them and consider healthy responses.

_____

_____

_____

KEEY LEADERSHIP

I AM WELL:
IMPROVING THE WELL-BEING OF LEADERS

The emotional tax of leadership and teamwork is often a heavy burden for leaders, especially women. Enduring the weight of responsibilities during uncertainties, in the face of chaos, or in psychologically unhealthy environments is cumbersome. This journey requires a deeply rooted sense of self-awareness that places significant emphasis on the physical, mental and spiritual well-being of oneself.

I give myself permission to be human; just as I give others permission to do the same.

My health dictates if and how I am able to show up.

As such, my physical, mental and spiritual well-being is my top priority.

Sustainable growth is the fruit of positive investments,
Of which I make intentional effort to engage.
I do right, knowing right will double in return.
Wellness is a reflective journey and is the catalyst for my leadership potential.
I am in tune with my burnout capacity,
And value when help is needed.

My defined outlets, are critical in overcoming stress and anxiety.

I work daily to develop my spiritual balance allowing me to rest well in times of distress.

I am whole, healthy and attentive to what I consume.

Internal dialogue is my greatest source of inspiration ,

So as to not allow the fear of the unknown to manipulate my actions.

I am well... I am secure...I am strong.

I am **KEEY!**

REFLECTIONS:

1. Having healthy outlets is crucial for current and aspiring leaders. What do you do to maintain a healthy lifestyle?

   _____

   _____

   _____

2. Does your organization have a health and wellness program? What do they offer and what benefits have you not taken advantage of?

   _____

   _____

   _____

3. For the next 30 days what type of lifestyle change can you commit to, to improve your physical and mental health?

_____

_____

_____

LEADING IN UNCERTAIN TIMES:
THE POWER OF KEEY LEADERSHIP
CONCLUSION

"We're here for a reason. I believe a bit of the reason is to throw little torches out to lead people through darkness."
—Whoopi Goldberg

As I draw this book to a close, I want to give attention to an extraordinarily critical phase in our global climate. In an effort to maintain complete transparency, I must admit that I have been somewhat bothered by the delay in drawing this project to a close. I just couldn't figure it out; however, today, I am moved to focus on the authenticity of its complete manifestation in this moment. During this time.

At present, our nation is experiencing a sense of stillness at the helm of a global health pandemic. It is unlike anything we've ever experienced in this generation, and, as a result, forced confinement to our homes has afforded me the opportunity to bring this lingering project to its conclusion. No previously written account of any historical event could have prepared me, or any of us, for this instance in time.

To this end, I am moved to reflect upon the many leaders across the world who are attempting to guide the masses during such uncertainty. The speed by which change is managed is purely mind-blowing. The way we now function as a society can only be described as unimaginable, making this work, whose purpose all along was to force critical self-reflection, more profound.

In the blink of an eye, critical decisions have transformed the operations of entire industries. Government leaders at the national, state and local levels have advanced serious mandates in an effort to manage the infiltration of a disease that is rapidly consuming human life. Healthcare executives are leading a frontline force of professionals who are not only working to manage an unknown intruder, identified as COVID-19, but doing so under remarkable circumstances. School leaders have been forced to restructure the educational system at all levels. As the demand for basic life necessities is often exceeding the available supply, grocery store workers have risen as our nation's unsung heroes. The economic devastation is rapidly increasing as unemployment becomes certain for many with the forced closing of small businesses and decreased revenue for larger ones.

Working remotely and technological operatives have become our new norm. In this moment, our homes have become sources of education academies for our children, home offices for working parents, recreational zones for physical activities, worship centers for spiritual deposits, and entertainment hubs for any activities that we creatively design due to the enforced mandate to quarantine as a nation. All these are efforts to systematically control the impact of a disease that has already obliterated other countries in places like China and Italy.

In this same moment, we have also entered into a modern day Civil Rights movement. An eruption in the ongoing struggle for social justice and the fight against systemic racism has manifested relentlessly with the recent murder of George Flyod, among countless others. A very public, but not uncommon influx of radical behaviors toward people of color has ignited a renewed frustration within our society. In this moment, the gaps, the inequalities, the inequities, the divisiveness that has saturated the fabric of our American culture for generations, has gained traction in a way that we've not experienced in modern times. There seems to be an awakening within industries across the country being forced to address their commitment to mitigating what many are calling a pandemic in itself. Leaders are leading amid social distancing and social injustices.

We are leading, guiding, and existing in different times. Times that have forced leaders in every facet of the word to shoulder the burden and responsibility of doing the best we can with the resources and information available in the moment. It is indeed a unique and dynamic period that calls for a greater sense of awareness at every stage of the KEEY Leadership Development Model for Exceptionality and Excellence. Moreover, it is a time that will define the legacy of leaders for years, even decades, to come. With this comes an inevitable call to action challenging leaders to remain as deeply introspective and authentic as possible.

It is also important to illustrate the full sense of our current climate, recognizing the seemingly oxymoronic moments of pureness and sweetness that comes from the gift of stillness. For years, we've challenged our leadership in an overzealous society that worshipped revenue over relationships and positioning over purpose. Yet, in many instances during this time, we are experiencing the beauty of servant leaders who are advocating for self-care, social justice and the needs of people over production. We are finding deep inspiration in the collective concern for humanity as we are all saddened by the lives directly impacted and the concern for what may lie ahead. And while we may all be managing differently, there seems to be acknowledgement for the increased need for grace and compassion. I think we can all agree that there exists a powerful awakening in this realization.

So, what happens from here?

The Keey Leadership Development Model for Exceptionality and Excellence serves as a foundational framework for leaders during times of both certainty and uncertainty. Shifting your mindset and embodying a certain level of personal consciousness is paramount to the process of staying committed to doing the work. While this project does not directly address the implementation or execution of tools, resources, and systems, it does set the stage by facilitating critical reflection around behaviors and perspectives.

Now, more than ever before, leadership legacies are driven by one's ability to not only navigate personal development but the influences that one's actions, decisions, and work will have on others and entire teams. As such, affirming and reflecting will only take us so far. What we choose to do in our moments of opportunities will have the greatest impact on our continued development as a leader.

In the blink of an eye, much like what is being experienced today, the reflections will turn into real life, on-the-job training. So, whether you are a current or prospective leader, you have hopefully been empowered to learn and lead, not simply in thought but in practice. My hope is that you have, in some way, informed a burning desire to change your behaviors.

Assuming you have fully committed to answering the reflection questions at the end of each affirming section and have engaged in critical conversations with your teams, what you now have is a strong foundation for influencing programming, processes, practices and even policies. You've identified problems, challenges, and areas of improvements. The next step is to evaluate your priorities and create action plans toward improvement!

You will not get it right every time, but what you can get right is your intention—the intention to be better at all three levels of the Keey Leadership Development Model. One thing is certain: with an emphasis on one's self (#iamKEEY), others (#youareKEEY), and our collective functioning as a team (#weareKEEY), regardless of the climate or culture, your legacy as a leader will be one of **EXCELLENCE** and **EXCEPTIONALITY**!

With that, may you always *BELIEVE TO LEAD*, and I'll see you on this forever developing journey, as the development never ends. Remember leader... **#iamKEEY, #youareKEEY, #weareKEEY.**

ABOUT THE AUTHOR

Wykesha (a.ka. Dr. Wy) is the founder and CEO of Keey Group, LLC, a leadership, learning, and development agency. Through coaching and training services, she helps current and aspiring leaders overcome skill deficits by aligning professional development plans with strategic business goals. She speaks on the power of leadership, executive presence and diversity, inclusion, and equity.

Having started her teaching career in the K-12 sector before transitioning into corporate leadership and strategic business development, Wykesha is an innate teacher that leverages connection and inspiration to pierce the actions of her clients. She maintains a passion for helping others not only learn but apply corporate principles while building their capacity as leaders and change agents.

She has trained thousands of leaders across various sectors including healthcare, education and non-profit. Her first published book, **BELIEVE TO LEAD** is a written illustration of her unshakable belief in the power of words. **BELIEVE TO LEAD** offers a collection of transformative reflections and thought-provoking considerations designed to shift the mindsets of current and aspiring leaders.

Her commentary in her weekly email series, Keey News: The Secret Sauce to Promotion and Productivity and Keey

Konversations a video podcast platform, offers her followers the perfect blend of inspiration, motivation and strategy.

Wykesha resides in the Houston area with her husband Steven, and son, Zaire. She can be reached at www.keeygroup.com or www.wykeshahayes.co

Made in the USA
Middletown, DE
11 March 2025